Dear Lesley,

CW00662689

The Room Between Us

Enjoy the book,

Denise x.

The Room Between Us

Denise Saul

First published 2022 by
Liverpool University Press
4 Cambridge Street
Liverpool
L69 7ZU

British Library Cataloguing-in-Publication data
A British Library CIP record is available

ISBN 978-1-80085-485-7 softback

Typeset by Carnegie Book Production, Lancaster
Printed and bound in Poland by Booksfactory.co.uk

i.m. of Eris.

Full many a flow'r is born to blush unseen,
And waste its sweetness on the desert air.

Thomas Gray, Elegy Written in a Country Churchyard

Contents

The Room Between Us

There you are, beside the telephone stand,
waiting for me in a darkened room
when I force open the white door.
There you lie, behind it.

I never found out why you grabbed
a pewter angel instead of the receiver
when you tried to call me that morning.
I give up trying to lift you from the floor

as the room is no longer between us.
You point again to the Bible, door, wall
before I whisper, *It's alright, alright,
now tell me what happened before the fall.*

Stroke (n) Old English *strācian* 'caress lightly', of Germanic origin; related to Dutch streek 'a stroke'. German *streichen* 'to stroke', also to strike. Act of hitting or striking someone or something, a blow. Part of a written or printed character. The rhythm to which a series of repeated actions are performed. In swimming, the movement of arms or legs. The sound made by a striking clock.

One

Step back now and look again at the femur.
Turn the bone upright and it is a glyph,
a perfect representation of the number one.

The research team names her part-skeleton
Australopithecus afarensis.
More shovels arrive in the morning.

The next day, workers dance to The Beatles'
'Lucy in the Sky with Diamonds'.
They drink a bottle of Shiraz; they christen her Lucy.

I raise a glass of Tej over the Hadar site and sniff
forest honey that grandmother mixed
with gesho leaves to make wine.

Grave-soil and termites fell from her mouth:
because her body was covered in skin, hard as flint,
she sometimes called herself Stone-Dress.

Grandmother wore black obsidian,
even though the desert cracked beneath her feet.
The belt was carved from the upper delta

and an emerald stream ran down her back.
When she carried a bag of chicken bones,
she clapped and chanted *sangoma, sangoma, sangoma.*

Grandmother placed the bones on a shrine
but could not read what they said.
I begged her not to leave the village.

The White Room

There is a moment for meditation when the doctor leads me into the room with table, bed and cupboard. When he leaves, I look out of the small window. There's a view of other windows unknown. I never thought I'd make peace with noise: chimes of the midnight bell, traffic, low-flying planes remind me that God is a never-ending-white ceiling. I look at the right hand that does not move on the cushion and I name it Paula. The clenched fingers look like a woman's head and this is where I locate a mouth in this small fist.

First Conversation

We talked for a few minutes about the memory book.

I sometimes thought that my birthday did not matter.

I hold up the photo of a white and black dress. You call black *a thing* by way of distinction.

The left eye is confined to a single colour. You forget everything that borders on white.

What you leave out is everything. You look away and close your eyes.

This happened and this happened and then this.

Left-Hander

I was trying to get her to explain what she wanted to wear.

Perhaps writing is the order of remembering.

She tried to draw what she wanted to wear.

The right-hander writes with the left hand.

She has written 'table' twice to recognise the difference. She leaves alone the letter 'a'.

I see a word among the doodle of lines. Again, I remind her to put down the pen.

There was more to be done. I saw her look at my drawing on the page.

I guess you get to a point where writing does not matter.

Minor Variations

She squeezed my wrist which meant I must carry on talking.

There are two major hand gestures and three combined signs.
I use two minor variations to tell her that I understand.

The same fingers that confer a blessing can point to the
window.

No two hands are alike. The left hand holds the affected right
arm.

What she leaves out describing are the days of the week.

She points too much but no-one has told her to stop.

House of Blue

There is something detached about this colour
which stands for the morning sky.
It contains everything and yet nothing.
At the House of Blue (which takes its name
from the blues), I rattle the sistrum
until the villagers run from the prayer-house
to see the clouds above Lake Tana.

They discovered when I was almost
seven that I could make rain fall
when I played the sistrum.
That year, the farmers looked at books
and magic scrolls to read the weather.
The local herdsman threw a bucket down
a well and heard it hit the bottom.

It was not far from here – at the brazier's
shop – where the smith pounded out
a strip of copper on his anvil.
Once I had listened to the pitch between notes
made by metal and hammer, I returned
to the House of Blue and carved
a sistrum handle from acacia.

At intervals, I attached five discs
to each of the traverse wires.
When I played *Apocalypse of Gregorios* or
Song of Baruch and added blue notes,
the discs jingled together.
I even noticed that the first sound
was twice as long as the second.

Think of a barley field when a woman plants
seeds for next summer, she sits
on grass to take possession of the earth.
The need for water stops her listening
to what is happening in this village.
Note the wind that carries husks across a stream
while the same plough rests in the yard.

The Bride Stripped Bare

After Marcel Duchamp

I am afraid of spiders and their desiring soul.
　　　　The arachnid blossoms, opens out, blooms
whenever its black body spins another web.
　　　　This mandala of silk is the undertaker.

Spiders run across the door.
　　　　One end of gossamer stretches, drawn
not from them but from their not-them.
　　　　The bedroom smells of dampness in corners.

Yet, this is the way I notice men:
　　　　priest, gendarme, warden, night watchman.

Instructions For Yellow

Saul's diary entry for September 2014: *I feel nothing from the sunlight that falls on my face.*

It is impossible that we will talk about it again.

A person in a room is affected by the colour of the walls.

The yellowness we see in the garden is not a daffodil.

She did not want us to wear black at the wake.

I can't recall who was silent first.

The surface of every body is affected by colour.

And yellow will look the most vivid against a dark background.

I thought she whispered something about the room but she wanted to say –

Clopidogrel

I was talking about the doctor or you were. I can't recall who
spoke first even though I said *clopidogrel* and you said *cabbage*.
In the afternoon, you mentioned *cardigan* and did not budge
from this word.

Nightingale House

that the woman disappeared from a house
named after the nightingale that sang
to passersby when it sat on the fence;
that the woman left behind a wardrobe
full of navy dresses and lace-up
shoes paired into neat rows of
blackness under the table
and there was no note to explain
where she went or the reasons why
she did not return to her bed
that was unslept in for weeks but
because of her disappearance,
her passing out of sight or departure,
the absence was gradual, first the voice
diminished into stillness,
a kind of letting go,
and on the dressing-table sat
a wallet of loose change;
that the woman left behind the scent of
Oil of Olay on her pillow
and rose oil on a pair of gloves;
I can tell you about the tapping
of wings against a hard object,
perhaps the window
while the curtains are drawn to let
light enter but even its light cannot
enter every corner of the room
and in the afternoon, a shadow falls
from dresses in the wardrobe,
that slips further away by the hour.

A Daughter's Perspective

When morning arrives, the radio stops speaking. Now, instead of hearing my mother speak from one, infinitely distant (and divine) point of view, further points of view are included in our conversation.

If I stand in front of the window and look at her wheelchair, the person in front of me seems to be smaller the closer she is.

I rub handcream into the back of her hand, starting at the wrist and working away from the heart. The nurse told me that it was better to massage away from the heart and not towards it. My mother opens her left hand and I pour some cream in her palm. She massages the back of my hand. I talk to her about work, neighbours and when she would be coming home.

A representation of a scene is often one simple conversation.

I asked the physiotherapist about walking with a cane. In the beginning, I thought she said that walking was possible. Even though I asked her before about leg supports, she said *never* and *wheelchair*. But since my question did not produce an answer, I repeated it. She stood still looking around the room as though she had never been here. On the second visit, I did not expect an answer from her because I had asked the same question twice.

In the evening, I read Paul Broca's *Mémoires d'Anthropologie*. My mother recites sentences from the left hemisphere: *In the mindfulness of listening, Sundays at home at home.*

Lotus Woman

Instead of gazing at the pond below,
Woman steps on yellow petals

stuck to the soles of her tiny feet.
The water is covered with leaves

which almost hold the sunlight;
while she is as big as a lotus flower.

Woman does not look at the sky,
just the tall shadow of herself

she pulls across the pavement.
Again, there are no bees to greet her

when she steps out of the pond,
only the steady hum of locusts.

On the way home, once Woman gets
on the village-bus, she counts

the stops because she fears
long roads of imlah trees.

Here it's hard walking beneath
rows of adey abeba bushes.

If you see Woman, touch her face.
It is the sun, the entire day itself.

Werehyena

Have a seat. No-one's sitting here.
This wedding's the same as the next one:
buffet, dancing and more cake.
You look like a blacksmith I knew
 back in Axum but we're here now in London

so he would be older than you.
 He made necklaces, gates,
sometimes the odd ring
and he always wore a silver chain.
Yes, he had a pet hyena.

It imitated the human voice
 and at times this blacksmith would go out
 to look for his pet in the backyard.
Well, the hyena smelled of hooves and beetles.
The blacksmith left the village one night.

Just like that.
A neighbour who was also my aunt said
one evening she saw two hyenas
 scavenging among the rubbish bins.
One wore a silver chain around its neck.

The odd evening, when I've drunk too much
and close my eyes, I sometimes see
the blacksmith wearing iron shackles.
 I offer him a beer before
asking him to sit down.

The Viewing

Behind another brown door into a windowless room,
Julie the director removes the lace veil
and maps her fingers on my mother's cheek.

Perfect skin, so smooth. No wrinkles, she says
as I walk around the room to view the off-white
dress and beret covered with cream pearls.

I want to tell my mother about how she still holds light,
and that this is the last day of seeing each other.
Julie says she spent the afternoon reading aloud

the horoscopes page from the daily newspaper.
I thank Julie for sitting with her as she always does.
No trouble at all. Virgo? she asks.

Standing by the table, I bend over my mother again
to take in the smell of Floris rose perfume.
No, Libra, I tell her. *Libra.*

In The Same House

Back in the city, two women lived in an Edwardian house. They wore matching dresses not because they enjoyed wearing the same clothes but because they forgot about the other dresses. There was no need to meet on any occasion which confused the neighbours who thought they were the same person. The women never visited each other because they lived on different floors. They phoned each other regularly to chat about shoes and hats and loneliness. Nothing is ever said of the twins who live in the house.

Someone Walked Into A Garden

He's the same one who gave us the Word and took it away
when we sat in the garden where bindweed climbed the wall.
A bracket of cowslips gathered under the dogwood. This was
where we heard him count seven days into a week. We saw
someone who looked like you and when she turned around,
it was me talking to myself. And I have dreamt this before,
someone who walked into a garden. I know it's you when I
talk with the god of roses; I have dreamt this often.

Observation

From the front room, she looked at the roses. Her body leant towards the left side of the leather armchair. I would have to reposition her right leg on the foot-rest. The sky was unclear with rain clouds. I wondered if she was bored with me or the television. She waved to me and I waved back.

The Meeting

The neurologist told me to have a cup of tea in the family meeting room.
He said, *As you are the main carer* at the start of each sentence.

The women hid their tongues when men did not listen to them.
The women in their beds cried to the nurses.

My questions did not produce simple answers.
It was Monday which meant that another week had started.

The women answered questions with their feet and eyes.
I looked for comfort at my sister but she was reading the leaflet.

The women closed their mouths because shoulders could speak for them.
As he spoke, I kept my eyes fixed on his face.

It might have helped us to know this last night, but perhaps it would not have.
We looked at the second MRI image. He reminded me about the cup of tea.

Of Glass

A nurse sat on the cushion which I thought was unnecessary because it was not her seat and I wondered if her feet perched on leg-rests disturbed me because she could walk. I raced a recliner in a local park. She worked in a clinic but had never pushed one around London which saddened me. I did not need imagination but the nurse said that she had imagination and could see herself sitting in one position as the cushion was comfortable. She knew about wheelchairs. Her aunt sat in one for three years. *They think that they're made of glass. Too afraid to lean forward.* I watched her put on her sandals and stand up. *Have you ever watched how she sits?* she asked. *Have you ever taken her to the cinema? Now, that's an interesting place.*

Stone Altar

I am not sure how the stone travelled
from British Guiana but the story goes
my mother brought it to England to remind her
of a passing like the way one remembers
the flight of a bird by keeping its feather.
What I thought was limestone was chalk
passed down from grandmother Frances
found among other stones in a black handbag
pushed to the back of a cabinet.
That autumn I asked my sister to tell me about
the stone when I sifted through the possessions.
When chalk gave away some dust, she held it
up to the light and told me about
other things in a world of decay.
It seemed easy enough for her to
wipe away the dust from her fingers.
No-one receives what they truly want.
It took me a while to understand all of this
when I placed the chalk on an altar
next to blue kyanite stones I collected.

On Sitting

Even the wheelchair carried her presence in its arms and back.

From Upstairs

I woke up in another room where a dream-catcher hung over the bed and photos of myself gazed at the table covered with tarot cards. I picked up a mirror to see the room and noticed that clocks in this house didn't all keep the same time. The woman from upstairs who wore a white dress sat down at my table saying *I know what you are thinking* and held my hand while she stared at the cards. She asked me if I had any questions but added she could not predict the future for there was no future. The mirror's surface cleared and the clock on the mantelpiece was the first to stop when she got up to leave in the morning.

Visitation

It's hard for a mother to leave and that's why I did not wipe her footsteps from the hall so that she could return home as I knew she would hurry back to smell the pot of lilies in the front room and look at herself in the mirror now covered with a white sheet.

Riddles

First Riddle

Let the stairwell be made as dark as possible. You are here to forget everything that borders on light. Uneven walls and polished floor give way to the window. On a day like this one, you call on me to unlock doors. Let my turning remind you of a town you left behind.

Second Riddle

Some mornings, she wishes away hours on my clock of seeds. I am here to remind the daughter of everything that is white. Petals from the same dandelion appear different but are the same. She has never learnt the art of letting go.

Third Riddle

Once I peeled a Gala apple, not for myself, and made sure each slice was small enough for a mouth that could not open. I cut away the skin and dug out its core just as she liked it but even then she could not eat. She held me with care as though I was made of fire.

Apollo Maison Street

Apollo Mason was a philanthropist who gave away
his land to the people of Golden Grove.
This great-grandfather emigrated from Barbados
with money from the sale of sugar plantations
and built a new village in British Guiana.
He reared pigs in pens, restored the local church roof,
donated money to orphans, resolved disputes
between neighbours and more than once held
community meetings under the old tamarind tree.
Born after his departure, I never knew him.
A government official named a street in his memory
but chose to misspell his family name.
In the fields, the villagers celebrated
his legacy and many pigs were slaughtered.

Surrender

I have grown tired of combing mother's unkempt hair. I do not know how to plait and the house is in a mess. Rather than using a comb, I pull my fingers through her hair. I tell mother to bend her head forward, *You have to lean forward if you want me to comb your hair.* Mother tilts her head back because she does not want to surrender to anyone.

Hemianopia

You are holding The National Enquirer. The first page disappears.

The mind fills a blind spot with informed fiction.

An illusion shows the world as it really is. The left eye uses this trick to great effect.

A blurry room is often interpreted as moving.

The consultant recommends focusing on a blank wall to still motion. As we turn our heads, the world is unstable around us.

I stand up to show her that I'm still here.

No Word For Blue

She who is quiet is boring company.

I had my ears pierced for the first time at the age of seven and, as I grew, my mother added hoop after hoop. The stretched lobes enhanced my neck.

My mother's ring has no beginning and no end. I donated it to a charity shop. A month later a friend returned the ring in a recycled box.

In colour theory, green is complementary to red. I watch a ladybird meditate on the grass.

Homer had no word for blue; he referred to the sea as dark. I wonder whether the sea exists or if it's just a place where the beach ends.

One is only a number, different from others except by coming first. All things are really one.

A Prayer That May Be Said
Before She Wakes

Thy will be done. Will you not teach me
how to kneel in the temple of a garden?
There is no morning prayer for us.
O father, you bring me back to a place
where I must wake each morning.
How I feel some belief in closing my eyes
but find days of stillness and turbulence
in the line 'Thy will be done' when I cannot
walk away from the call of a magpie.
I can do nothing but listen to His words.
Hallowed be thy name. He says magpies
rest wreaths of yarrow on fallen birds.
Thy will be done. If I say, So be it,
there is only one person who hears.
The ear relieves itself by hearing
different birdsongs forced upon it.
I have enough March-like days to sit on
a garden bench. I am cold all over.

Clematis

Whose firmament do they look up to
when foretelling Surrey weather?
They cling to what was never theirs
and yet the crowns are rewarded with
delicate things of solemn purple.
Unlike vine suffered to dry
on the iron fence, clematis clings
to bricks and rinse of sunlight.
Thankless they insist that the earth is theirs.

Golden Grove

i.m. Aubrey

Unbearable as night from which sleep comes,
you are everywhere at once: in the wind
on sunken earth   in stilling water.
I carry your heavy urn to Golden Grove
where tamarind trees emerge as woods.

The dream holds back day from night.
And you, a wanderer, could not wait
to leave rain behind in our city.
You will now become a thousand things:
scent of jasmine   salted air   troubling light.

Heirlooms

I

The rosary is white; no more white
than the candle on my mother's altar
and yet this heirloom turns out to hold
a replica of the cross carried by a man
who was not afraid of dying.
On days locked down, I wear her
crosses for the rule is always to pass on
objects we no longer need.

II

I begin each day with signing a cross on my body. Mother's
rosary is made up of decades. A decade is one Our Father
followed by ten Hail Mary's and a Glory Be. It is better to say
one decade in the morning than ten decades in the evening. By
chanting five, I complete one circuit of beads. As I chant, I think
about my brother's days. There are almost five decades to think
about when I count the bead-touchings.

III

I wear the silver cross around my neck
but it may be many years before
it can be passed on again.
I once asked myself what would it feel like
to pray before an object
when its nature was hidden from me.
For a god who does not reveal
his true intentions is not a god at all.

IV

I end some days with holding what was never mine: Anima
Christi, novenas, Gucci reading glasses, *Book of Psalms*,
Guyanese gold bracelet, Saint Christopher's pendant, book of
prayers for the living.

The Eye Can Miss So Much

I watch him wake up from his seventh dream. It is Sunday so he wears a gold and black Versace dressing-gown and brocade slippers. Again, he counts himself back to sleep for in the dream, he sits in a bottomless well. This term at college, he is teaching fashion design for beginners. Tonight he thought that he met an angel who carried him back to bed. He takes off his wet dressing-gown. The eye can miss so much in a dark space without the brightness of a lamp.

Status Epilepticus

There is a room full of night sky that she will meet
and if I could only hold her hand to let her know
this too will pass into a wayward jolt of electric blue.
I observe her head forced through a crown of stars
and when she goes again, minutes of darkness follow.
Even Socrates knew of that entranced departure
during a morning's worth of blackness.
Some days, she rises in this way and every evening
she must move towards a blackout of the heavens.
Another minute; arm knocks over a vase of floribunda.
It is time for the left leg to bend and straighten.
Another minute; then see how gravity seizes her.
I try to bring her back before she leaves behind
indigo walls and odour of roses which is everywhere.

How The Crystal Healer Brings Light
Back To A Body

To live in the shadow of crystals
I must first know their names.
Because rose quartz chooses to move what
it touches, I place the crystal under her feet.
I have learnt how to channel light from
a crystal into her head, arm and leg.
On Friday, her eyes told me
she was now ready to climb the heavens.
For a mother to leave the ruined sanctuary
of this house, I say, *Let us dedicate rose quartz*
to cleansing the body – allow her to leave
with ease, without water, with frankincense.
Even Jacob dreamt of the way
to the heavens as by a broken ladder.
I remember how my brother stood at the foot
of a ladder in the yard but could not climb it.
When I look out of the window,
there is the light I cannot keep.
In a house like this, I repeat the names
of those I serve – celestite, Eris, turquoise.
Yet again, god shape-shifts of his own
accord to rocks of severity and mercy.

The Eternal

G F Watts, The All-Pervading, *Tate Gallery*

When the scryer holds a sphere, eyes are closed
as there is no need to see everything at once.
A face brought to its cold surface stares back at her.
She sees a father walk the immeasurable expanse of
nothingness since her gaze is measured and hard.
Who could have thought of reading a ball of leaden
glass for those who believe in the eternal spirit?
At times, the reflection of herself is mistaken
for galaxies and stars of the cosmos.
Clouds turn into many earthquakes
and the ground becomes an aurora borealis.
Even now, she does not see the sky or where
the earth begins as they are of equal dark intensity.
And it is not possible to count the many
faces that come to her since the eyes cannot
always focus on another man's fate.
Some faces seem to be alike in this evening's mirror.
They peer through a dim and narrow
window into the brightness of mist before them.
When she turns the globe to scry its shadows,
her father changes to other visions – a lost boy,
and then a wooden door that cannot shut.
Perhaps this is what Watts meant when
seeing the glass drop of a chandelier in
a rented house, he drew the hooded figure
with a green orbuculum on her lap.
And when the reading ends, the seer gazes only
at the reflection of a woman held within the sphere.

A Woman Travels In Search Of Sound

On the move again this time to Surrey
but I could not take with me
all the plants my family left behind.
The row of simple petunias made
their last appearance this summer.
All the plants I hear them, and the quieter
they are, the more I hear them.
The breaking sound of twigs comes to me
as I clear away leaves under bushes.
A helicopter overhead circles the house –
its presence breaks the many silences of grass.
I hear all the registers of flowers.
Newton was not the first to make
a connection with the ways of green,
its part-yellow and part-blue.
Here, the petunias follow mother's
ordering of size rather than of importance.
Even with the final walk from the side-gate
to the removal van, I hear the unequal
division of sound between the tread
on a concrete path and quiet
water pooling beneath the gutter.

Retrograde

When mercury moves backwards in mid-August,
I am reminded of the smallest things like that warm
night when you let a headscarf fall on the floor
but could not pick it up though you held
my hand. What I said to you before opening
a back door to the patio, I could not remember.
I was convinced a summer breeze would cool us down.
What bothered me most was I heard someone
call your name from the yard but you could not see anyone.
There have been other strange nights, none as dim,
when I stood in the rain to watch earthworms
break up soil, knowing the earth makes us small.
Over here mercury seemed to move away from us
in the beginning, but in truth, it never moved at all.

Acknowledgements

I would like to thank Deryn Rees-Jones for her careful and thoughtful attention towards the poems.

Page 2 – fragments from Oxford English Reference Dictionary and Collins English dictionary.

'A Woman Travels In Search of Sound'. Words from *Colour: A Visual History* by Alexandra Loske.

Thanks to the editors of the following magazines and pamphlets where these poems or versions of them first appeared:

House Of Blue (Rack Press), *New Humanist*, *Too Young, Too Loud, Too Different* (Corsair), *Qorrax* (Vanguard Editions), *Try To Be Better* (Prototype), *Oxford Poetry*, *Poetry London*, *POEM*, *Magma*.

'Minor Variations' was a commission for Dial-A-Poem project funded by AHRC and Nottingham Trent University.

'Nightingale House' is dedicated to Marie Gregory.

I am also deeply indebted to Mona and MPK. All my gratitude to Mimi Khalvati.

Thanks to the staff at Aphasia Re-Connect (formerly Connect) and Lauren Marks.

And finally to Eris, thank you for the poems.